FUNDRAISING MISTAKES THAT BEDEVIL ALL BOARDS (AND STAFF TOO)

A 1-Hour Guide
to Identifying and Overcoming
Obstacles to Your Success

Printed in the United States of America

ISBN 978-1-889102-40-5

10 9 8 7 6 5 4 3 2

This text is printed on acid-free paper.

Copies of this book are available from the publisher at discount when purchased in quantity for boards of directors or staff.

Emerson & Church, Publishers
15 Brook Street • Medfield, MA 02052
Tel. 508-359-0019 • www.emersonandchurch.com

Library of Congress Cataloging-in-Publication Data

Grace, Kay Sprinkel.
  Fundraising mistakes that bedevil all boards (and staff too) : a 1-hour guide to identifying and overcoming obstacles to your success / by Kay Sprinkel Grace. -- Rev. ed.
      p. cm.
  ISBN 1-889102-40-7 (pbk. : alk. paper)
  1. Fund raising--United States. 2. Nonprofit organizations--United States--Finance. 3. Social service--United States--Finance. I. Title.
  HV41.9.U5G713 2009
  658.15'224--dc22
                                    2009034114

Kay Sprinkel Grace

FUNDRAISING
MISTAKES THAT
BEDEVIL
ALL BOARDS
(AND STAFF TOO)

A 1-Hour Guide to
Identifying and
Overcoming
Obstacles to
Your Success

Emerson
& Church
PUBLISHERS

This book is dedicated to my late mother,
Marian Boyles Sprinkel, who taught me that
you cannot accomplish great things if you're afraid
to make a mistake. She is still my inspiration.

"Mistakes are the portals of discovery."

–James Joyce

CONTENTS

INTRODUCTION

1   Tax deductibility is a powerful incentive   15

2   Foundations and corporations are the   17
    biggest donors

3   Special events are the best way to raise money   19

4   People will give just because ours is a   21
    good cause

5   People will just find out about us   23

6   Donors are drawn to organizations in need   25

7   We'll attract funding because our hearts are   27
    in the right place

8   You have to be a household name to   29
    win support

9   You can secure big gifts by writing letters   31

10 Publicity raises money   33

11 People dislike giving   35

12 Big donors are different, they're not like us   37

13   People won't support a cause like ours   39

14   We can't raise big money – we don't know any   41
     rich people

15   Giving is largely a rational decision   45

16   Others are more comfortable asking for money   47
     than you

17   The state of the economy is key to fundraising   49

18   Wealth is what mostly determines a person's   51
     willingness to give

19   To secure a gift, saying just the right words   53
     is key

20   You don't have to give money yourself – your   55
     gift is your time

21   It's impolite to ask for a specific amount   57

22   Asking once a year is enough   59

23   Development staff, because it's their job, are   61
     more effective in asking

24   Fundraising consultants (and development   65
     officers) often bring with them a list of people
     to solicit

25   We can run this campaign on the cheap   67

26   Fundraising costs are a measure of our   69
     organization

27   You need to powerful board to have a successful   71
     campaign

28   Not everyone on the board has to be involved   73
     in fundraising

29   It's prudent to focus on large donors only   75

30   Estate gifts only come from big donors   77

31 You need a stable of annual donors to have a successful capital campaign   79

32 If you don't know how much a prospect can give, shoot for the moon   81

33 Some can't afford to give and shouldn't be asked   83

34 You need a feasibility study before launching a capital campaign   85

35 If you've been trained in asking at one organization, you needn't attend another agency's training   87

36 For those giving small gifts, a simple acknowledgment is fitting   89

37 If someone is already contributing to an organization similar to yours, asking her to give to you is poaching   91

38 Your goal in a major gifts or capital campaign is simply the amount of money you need   93

39 Consultants aren't needed if you have a fundraising staff   95

40 Nowadays, people want you to get to the point and ask – cultivation wastes time   97

41 If your early fundraising calls don't spark interest, chances are your cause isn't important enough   99

42 We can probably count on a few 'windfall' gifts   103

43 Fundraising is a lot easier once you get the hang of it   105

44 With so many causes raising money, the wells of philanthropy are drying up   107

A FINAL WORD   109

INTRODUCTION

In my decades of work with nonprofits, I have addressed many recurring mistakes that board members, volunteers, and staff make when raising money. The "aha!" that occurs when we fix the mistake is so transforming I thought I'd like to capture the top ones in this book.

Some mistakes are absolute (they are poor practice wherever you are and whatever you do); some are relative to your community or cause. If you find that only a handful of these apply to your situation, I believe you'll still find your fundraising improved.

My hope is that this book will be a useful tool for board members and staff alike. For board members, weary of lengthy training sessions or coaching, it will save you time.

As a guide for staff members just starting out, or those needing a boost in helping board members become more comfortable and effective in their fundraising role, its shortcut approach will be appealing.

Regardless of your role, I do hope what you're about to read will be informative, a bit fun, and, most importantly, helpful in advancing the cause to which you are committed.

Kay Sprinkel Grace *San Francisco, Calif.*
www.kaygrace.org
kaysprinkelgrace@aol.com

1

MISTAKE

Tax deductibility is a powerful incentive

I cringed when he said it.

We were all comfortably seated in the living room of one of our top prospects. As he listened carefully and nodded, we shared with him the vision for a new medical center. It would vastly improve the delivery of healthcare in the community. And his gift of $1 million would be key.

Everything was going extremely well. I could sense he was about to say yes.

And then my colleague chirped in. "And don't forget you can write this off," he said.

It was subtle, but if you watched his eyes, you could see how deflating our host found these words. Here, he was acting nobly, giving a sizable sum to enhance the lives of young and old alike. In his mind, he was returning some of the blessings he'd been given in his life.

My colleague, on the other hand, reduced it all to a monetary transaction.

"That's fine," our host said, trying to conceal his annoyance. "But about the boy in this picture, you're saying we don't have the equipment to treat him locally?"

The tax advantages of giving are motivating for some. But for most, they aren't a prime incentive.

Ironically, the very people we think of as most needing a tax break are often maxed out on their deductions. One generous university donor, setting up an estate gift, was told of the sizable tax advantage involved. She replied she'd have to live to 120 to realize all of the accrued benefits from her philanthropy (she was in her 80s at the time!).

To be sure, you'll want to understand the donor's circumstances well enough to know the tax ramifications. And be prepared to speak to them if asked. But don't lead off with talk about the IRS, unless the person you're asking has given you reason to.

Virtually any nonprofit can offer the identical tax advantage. But not every organization can match the donor's values and dreams as yours can.

Seek out the donor's true motivation, in your conversations with him and by reviewing any information you have about his giving. And then speak to that motivation in your presentation. Only in this way will you stoke his desire to support you.

Incidentally, anecdotal research done several years ago showed that on a list of 25 reasons why people give, "tax concerns" was number 16.

2

MISTAKE

Foundations and corporations are the biggest donors

Gifts from foundations and corporations, unlike those from individuals, are often widely publicized. That's why The Ford Foundation and Bank of America, and other foundations and corporations like them, enjoy the reputation for being the best source for large gifts, and why we expend so much energy soliciting them.

But if you look closely at American philanthropy, you'll see that giving by foundations and corporations accounts for less than 20 percent of all the money given each year to charitable organizations. The rest comes from individuals like you and me, either directly or through our estates. (Pity we don't have PR departments to broadcast our generosity.)

Even so, many a board member will persist in believing that foundations and corporations are the roads to riches. I, for one, think it's because grantseeking is typically spearheaded by staff who do the research, write the proposals, and follow up. Boards often defer to this kind of giving because, typically, they needn't get involved on a personal basis with asking.

But individuals are a vast and wonderful market. They don't have to consult a committee to make a gift. They can give without restrictions. They'll contribute more than once a year if so moved. They live in the community and are invested in the outcomes.

Don't overlook foundations and corporations; a balanced fundraising program should certainly include them. But focus your energy on individuals. The payoff will be far greater.

3

MISTAKE

Special events are the best way to raise money

At one time, special events seemed to be the best way to raise money. The blockbuster gala, netting $100,000, struck everyone as a quick fix for the annual fund.

The problem, we came to see later, was that most of our net figures didn't include "soft costs" like staff time. When these and other expenses were factored in, the net plummeted.

Regrettably, the lesson hasn't been learned by enough organizations. Calendars in most communities are so full that caring people could be at three events a week and, during the spring and fall, three events a night! One friend recently termed the event we were attending part of her "100 Days in May."

In my first job, I inherited a calendar in which there

were nine events of modest scale (domino tournament, tennis tournament) and one blockbuster (a summer symphony concert). In my youthful zeal, I added another big wine tasting party.

Then came our sobering year-end cost analysis. Not only was our net much lower than reported, but volunteer burnout (even with a large auxiliary) was spreading like a virus. So was staff burnout. Gradually we scaled back and began expanding our outreach to individuals for major gifts.

We keep falling into the special events trap for two reasons. They prevent us from having to approach our friends and colleagues for significant gifts (we can sell them tickets or a table of 10 instead). And – from the outside – they appear quick and easy. Put together an event. Open the doors. Have a good time. Count the money.

But if you've ever organized or chaired an event, you know how deceptive that is. You're better served devoting the same amount of time and people to cultivating those who can make large gifts.

View special events primarily as "friend raisers." Then, your expectations will be more realistic. And if and when you do host them, make sure your events complement your mission, and that your interaction with those who attend (donors and prospective donors) is part of your overall fundraising strategy.

4

MISTAKE

People will give just because ours is a good cause

I wish this were true. Just think how strong our community organizations would be and how much less time we'd have to spend raising money.

Regrettably, I've seen my share of good causes fail for lack of money.

One comes to mind immediately – an agency serving job-seeking women. Although their service was exemplary, and lives were lifted as a result, the agency foundered. That's because, like this group, yours can be the best cause in the world and still not raise money if:

1) You fail to involve the right people

2) You don't inspire trust

3) You neglect the 'harder' side of your mission: namely, delivering results in a cost-effective way.

In all but the extraordinary case (the South Asian tsunami and Hurricane Katrina come to mind) the people involved with the cause determine its ability to raise money.

An old fundraising adage still rings true: "People don't give to causes, they give to people who believe in causes."

Unless you, your CEO and staff, and your volunteers are committed to the mission, communicate its importance, and develop relationships with those who share your values, you won't attract substantial or long-lasting support.

But that's only part of the story. You still need an organization with integrity, that's well-run, whose impact can be quantified.

Today's donors are a demanding lot. Unless you meet these expectations, they'll simply go shopping for another cause that does.

5

People will just find out about us

When I hear organizations say they're the "best kept secret" in the community, I say that's too bad. Unless you need to keep your work out of the public eye – rare for the overwhelming majority of organizations – good publicity is your ally.

Believing that people will discover how wonderful you are without marketing yourself is akin to the 1940's Hollywood starlet who thought she'd be "discovered" by sitting at the soda fountain at Schrafts Drug Store. Maybe it worked for one or two, but as a career strategy, it was a failure.

We're a media-driven society, and even with tight budgets organizations must find ways to attract people's attention. You can't hide your light under the proverbial bushel and expect people to know yours is an organization that reflects their values and accomplishes what they want. Take the Philharmonia Baroque Orchestra, America's foremost period instrument ensemble. Some years ago, knowing it needed to convey a more contemporary image, the orchestra discarded its ornate branding and focused instead on what "PBO" could stand for other than the orchestra's name. Voila: Passionate, Brilliant, Original. Emerging from a spate of financial pressures, PBO didn't have thousands of dollars to market itself. But it used all of the volunteer, pro bono, and professional resources it could marshal, knowing that a new image was key to its long-term goals of increasing subscribers and attracting younger audiences.

The marketing campaign made brilliant use of eye-catching billboards showing the impish, animated, and superb music director, Nic McGegan, as someone who was anything but stuffy or stolid. Not long after, PBO attracted press coverage on a number of other fronts: the hiring of the new executive director, the successful completion of an endowment campaign, the launching of a new season, and the renewal of the beloved music director's contract.

The result? PBO is now understood, recognized, and supported as never before. All achieved with relatively limited resources.

Understand, publicity alone won't raise money (see Mistake #10). But it can effectively set the stage for you. Be less of a secret, and donors and prospects will be more informed – and receptive – when you call upon them.

6

MISTAKE

Donors are drawn to organizations in need

Decades ago, when the nonprofit playing field was less crowded, many people responded to a charity's neediness. Some of our organizations even portrayed themselves that way: shabby offices, amateurish publications, and seat of the pants financing.

All that has changed. Those who lament that money pours into great universities, major arts organizations, and other giant nonprofit enterprises rather than to those who really "need" it have to see the reason why: these organizations radiate success.

They are professional, good at reporting their impact, and offer opportunities for people to fulfill their charitable instincts and have their investment protected.

A message of desperation may work once. Or even twice. But more than a few community orchestras and social service organizations have faded from the horizon when their frantic pleas for money ultimately fell on deaf ears. Those who had bailed them out let loose of the bucket.

For years I've spoken of our need to put away the tin cup. To stop begging. But, unfortunately, the mentality lingers, in part because the very origins of many of our organizations were based on presenting themselves as charities in need of a handout.

We must move away from that.

Present your organization for what it is – dedicated, robust, visionary, making a difference in the community. Say to your prospects and donors: "Without you, fewer children will have nutritional meals. Without you, scores of seniors will lack a home where they're treated with dignity and respect. Without you, abused women will continue to be at risk and have fewer resources for rebuilding their lives."

In sum, let your supporters know that it's their compassion and generosity that make it all possible. Donors will be drawn to you. I guarantee it.

7

MISTAKE

We'll attract funding because our hearts are in the right place

In the beginning, people who practiced philanthropy as volunteers and staff were often called "do-gooders." It was enough then to do good: now we also have to do well.

No matter how sincere your intentions, it's a mistake to think they're enough to inspire people to give.

Metrics, transparency, accountability, return on investment – these are the words guiding donors today.

Even iconic organizations have been challenged. Post 9/11, the American Red Cross ruffled the feathers of its supporters when it failed to spend the millions that poured in *for* disaster relief *on* disaster relief.

Contrast that with Doctors Without Borders, which over the Internet sent urgent notices to donors to stop sending money for the great tsunami of 2005 because enough resources had been raised.

"Trust" continually emerges as the single greatest reason people give to an organization. "Credibility," "Impact," and "Careful stewardship of the gift" are cited as well. But we can only hold our donors' trust when we demonstrate that, while our heart's in the right place, so is our leadership, our measurable impact, and our bottom line.

Even when the economy is fragile, or rather, especially when the economy is fragile, people will continue to give to organizations that have integrity, fiscal stability, a vital mission, and a vision that articulates what the community will be like when the need is met.

Heart is still a huge factor in philanthropy and will always be so. But our efforts must combine the heart and the "head" if we hope to gain loyalty and ongoing support.

8

MISTAKE

You have to be a household name to win support

YMCA. Goodwill. Red Cross. Salvation Army. Habitat for Humanity.

Household names, yes. Or, as the marketers call them: brands.

But it's a mistake to think you have to be a household name to win support. We hide behind that idea when explaining why our annual or capital goals fell short, or why we failed to receive even a portion of the estate of one of our donors. It all went to the Salvation Army.

In my first development job, at a day treatment school for children with special needs, I was notified shortly after I began work that we had received an estate gift. The name of the donor wasn't in my files (BC, before computer), so I asked some of our long-time donor relations volunteers about him.

At first, no one remembered, but they had a system that in hindsight seems primitive: a shoebox filled with 3 x 5 cards of donors who had stopped giving. His card was in there. His last gift had been $25, given 10 years earlier.

Someone remembered he had a blind wife and they used to walk around our school campus. He once told one of the volunteers how his wife loved the sounds of the children.

The charitable portion of the estate was allocated among several groups: our organization and two household names – Braille Institute and Reader's Digest Books for the Blind. But we received the residue of the estate, making our final distribution nearly twice what the others received.

To him, we were more important than the household names.

Trust in a brand is important – we see that in purchases we make. But just like the "off brand" you try and find to be superior to the brand you've always used – your organization can distinguish itself among your donors through its programs, outreach to the community, stewardship of its donors, and perception as a true community partner.

9

MISTAKE

We can secure big gifts by writing letters

This is one of the biggest mistakes board members make and it happens all the time.

In fact, I recently heard of a letter asking for $3 million. Imagine. It seems the relationship between the asker and the asked was too strained for a personal meeting!

I'm not saying it can't be done. And there are instances when a letter is the right approach.

But for the most part big gifts are sought in person. The actual moment of asking is the end result of research, cultivation, dialogue, shared values, and – most importantly – the creation of a relationship.

Yet we persist in writing letters for a number of reasons.

First, and perhaps foremost, it means we don't have

to put ourselves on the line, and face the possibility of rejection or embarrassment.

Second, many people insist they can present the case more effectively in a letter (in which case it should be used as a warm-up for the visit with the prospective donor).

Third – and perhaps the only reason that justifies a letter – are circumstances that make a letter the *only* option: schedules, geography, illness, or the prospective donor demands the request in writing. But the fact that you know these conditions means you've had communication with either the prospect or her representative. That is critical.

If you're tempted to write a letter because you feel clumsy about asking or don't want to face possible rejection, work to overcome your own anxiety and misgivings.

Ask for coaching. Ask for a partner to go with you. Ask for a bromide if you must. But don't jeopardize your cause by surrendering to your own fears.

10

MISTAKE

Publicity raises money

Too often, we believe that just spreading the word will solve our funding problems. People will read about the good things we're doing and – bingo! – they'll send in fistfuls of dollars.

One organization I worked with was featured in a national magazine in which one of the people interviewed cited the amount needed for a new facility. The organization honestly expected to be flooded with gifts as a result. It didn't happen. A few gifts trickled in, but no significant outpouring.

Publicity is essential in building an image in the community. But it shouldn't be relied on as an avenue for fundraising. They are separate functions.

Raising awareness of your impact and the credibility of your organization is critical. Bus and bus shelter ads, articles in newspapers and magazines, a tasteful website that's user friendly, email alerts about your upcoming activities or advances you've made – all these contribute to your brand recognition. To the extent you can get such support on a pro bono basis, all the better.

But marketing does little more than pave the way for fundraising. You still have to get out there and ask. In fact, it is only when an individual you're soliciting says to you, "I'm making this gift because I recently read about your work," that you know your publicity has been effective.

By all means publicize yourself – vigorously in this media-conscious age. But keep in mind that publicity is merely a prelude – and a reinforcement – to the *personal overtures* essential to successful fundraising.

If you don't believe me, answer this simple question: When was the last time *you* sent a gift – a meaningful gift – in response to something you saw on TV or read in the paper?"

Case dismissed.

11

MISTAKE

People dislike giving

Although they may balk at the amount of the request or need a "gestation" period before agreeing to invest, most people do like to give. In fact, most feel true joy when giving.

I recall Denise – she gave the largest gift to our museum campaign. When the board invited her to a meeting to thank her personally, what struck everyone in the room was the joy and gratitude she expressed.

Moved to tears, Denise said how much the museum's mission meant to her, what a privilege it was for her to help fulfill this dream, and how honored she felt to be involved.

Her sentiments will surprise those who think fundraising is all about pressure, about talking someone into a gift they don't want to make.

Truth be told, pressure doesn't really work or, at best,

works one time and creates ill will. You can bet you'll be shunned if you use hard-sell tactics.

Now it is true that many times you'll have to identify just the right giving opportunity. And you may stumble once or twice.

I remember one university campaign when school officials kept striking out with Katherine. Over the course of a few months, they presented her with several possibilities for funding, but none piqued her interest. Nevertheless, they kept the relationship open, inviting Katherine to various events.

And it was at one of these events – a presentation by a group of undergraduate students – that Katherine began asking questions about how the students did their research and who funded them.

While undergraduate research was a priority for the campaign, no one had suggested it as an option for Katherine because she held a graduate (but not under-graduate) degree from the university.

But it turns out her graduate work had been largely built on work she'd done as an undergraduate. Katherine enthusiastically made a gift.

I can tell you from 30 years of frontline experience: most people enjoy giving. You just have to inspire them by asking in a way that connects their dream with yours and reflects what you've learned about their interests and style.

12

MISTAKE

Big donors are different, they're not like us

I often alter a quote from the lexicon of that great American philosopher, Pogo the Possum (a creation of the late cartoonist, Walt Kelly), who said, "We have met the enemy, and he is us." My version is: "We have met the donor, and he (or she) is us."

Giving cuts across all demographics. The people we approach are in fact a lot like us: many live next door, are in our kids' carpool, compete on the same golf course, and are waiting in the checkout line next to you. Ironically, some of them may look at us and want to bring us closer to an organization they care about.

Even those who do live in the gated community on the other side of town, or the penthouse apartment on the lake, still have common connecting points with us. They care about the same things, feel the same pain over a loss, and want to be part of the solution to a chronic community problem.

If, for example, I'm a board member from the middle class fighting to eradicate juvenile diabetes, and your daughter has been diagnosed with the disease, exactly how important is it that my financial assets pale next to yours?

We share the same hope to end this life-threatening disorder; it's what draws us together despite our socio-economic disparity.

Giving is a matter of the heart, and is inspired when reputable organizations connect with people who care. Reaching out to them with an invitation to make a difference, to join with you in combating a disease or building a school, will be the bridge between you and people from all corners of your community.

13

MISTAKE

People won't support a cause like ours

Children. Babies. Animals. We all know what gets the money and attention.

But if yours is a cause that makes people uncomfortable, one they'd rather not talk about, or one addressing issues with limited acceptance, then you might mistakenly think you can't raise money.

Not so.

I've worked with an organization that served adult survivors of incest. We raised money. I've worked with agencies focusing on domestic violence long before it was a mainstream issue, and they are thriving. I've worked with groups advocating for freedom in sexual preference, and they've expanded their donor rolls exponentially.

There is a simple window through which we need to

view all donors – those who support children, animals, survivors of domestic violence, and lesbian and gay rights – and that is: All philanthropy is based in values.

We know from research and from our own experience that people don't give to, join, or serve organizations whose values they don't share. Try as you might, you won't get a pro-choice advocate to give to a pro-life cause.

Still, while you may have a smaller constituency with unpopular or sensitive causes, often you'll have a more loyal backing because they are people who've experienced the issue in some way. What they lack in numbers, they make up for in passion.

Also, with increasing numbers of private and family foundations focusing on issues-based giving, many have one of these narrow or emerging causes as their focus.

If your cause isn't mainstream, don't despair – and don't make the mistake of thinking there's no support for you. The key is in finding imaginative links.

In the past, for example, you'd have been hard-pressed to interest men in domestic abuse issues. Undaunted, the Family Violence Prevention Fund approached who else? male athletes – a group conscious of its image *and* much admired by boys and young men. Who better to be "Coaching Boys Into Men" than these idolized baseball, football, basketball, and soccer players?

Engage those who are passionate, whether or not they have money. People who care will find the warm and fuzzy in your cause.

14

MISTAKE

We can't raise big money, we don't know any rich people

First, let's dispense with the idea that raising big money always depends on wealthy donors. Think Barack Obama. According to the *Washington Post*, Mr. Obama attracted six million gifts of $100 or less. The average donation was $80.

In the wake of such success, it's not surprising that many organizations are attempting to adapt his strategy of electronic outreach.

But let's keep our focus on traditional giving and assume the Internet won't produce such bounty for you.

That was certainly the case with a church campaign I oversaw for $12 million in a woefully impoverished area. It was clear from the outset that none of the people involved knew anyone wealthy.

But we didn't let that stop us.

Through a carefully developed plan that engaged the board as well as a community committee of corporate, civic, and union leaders who were drawn by the importance of giving this area of the city a boost, we identified people who cared about the church's work. And they responded generously – one anonymous donor gave $1 million – because they shared our values.

We limit ourselves when we think that because we're a small organization, or serve a limited population, few will be interested.

It isn't the size of the organization that matters, it's the importance of the mission. When Project Open Hand was launched in San Francisco, an organization that brings meals to homebound people with HIV/AIDS, it was from the kitchen of the founder and the meals were delivered in friends' cars.

Although the group was tiny, and the founder didn't know many wealthy people, support poured in. Why? The need was great, and Project Open Hand was meeting it. The word got out, and people invested.

You don't need wealthy individuals in your data base to raise money. But without them, there are two imperatives facing you:

1) You must get your message out and relate the impact of what you're doing to the broader needs of the community, and

2) You must think of ways to identify and approach those who do have money.

In the case of the church, their work with the poor and indigent, as well as the large ethnic communities in the neighborhood, was attractive to the million-dollar donor whose own family, decades ago, had been a struggling immigrant family attending the church. Although Miguel and his family no longer lived in the area, the church had kept them informed through the years. When Miguel was approached, it didn't take many meetings for him to realize that although the community had changed, as had the needs of the immigrants, the mission and people were worthy of his investment.

If you don't know wealthy people, make no mistake: raising money is much harder and demands more imagination. But it's not impossible. With tenacity on the part of the board and the staff – and simultaneous outreach to many who can give small gifts – it can be done.

15

MISTAKE

Giving is largely a rational decision

If there's any transaction that engages the left and right brain more fully than making a charitable gift, I don't know of it.

Lean too strongly to one hemisphere or the other, and you jeopardize the gift.

Plans, budgets, blueprints, architectural models – these all appeal to a donor's rational side. They give comfort. They show your foundation is solid – and that's important.

But even the best laid plans, in and of themselves, won't elicit a gift. The donor has to feel an emotional tug as well. In his heart, he has to identify with your dreams and vision.

That's why it's always important to seek a balance when approaching donors.

Support your stories by statistics, and your statistics with stories. If, for example, you tell a donor you served 600 families last year, tell her about one of those families. Or, if you start by describing one of those families, be sure to let the donor know the story was played out 600 times in different ways.

Because so many organizations have abused the emotional side of giving (direct mailings with bashed baby seals, vivisected animals, starving children) countless people have inured themselves to exploitative appeals. Who can blame them?

But there's always a place for genuine emotion, and for storytelling, especially since ours is the business of improving and often saving lives.

Engage both hemispheres and even the most rational prospect will be touched.

16

MISTAKE

Others are more comfortable asking for money than you

Everyone thinks this. Others make it look so easy. But, believe me, they have the same anxieties as you.

Probably the best volunteer fundraiser I ever knew confessed to me that he still got nervous before a making a call. And here was a man who had secured gifts from hundreds of donors over 30 years.

But is it really different in other fields? We've all heard how even Tony award-winning actors have the butterflies before stepping onto the stage, and major league pitchers with the lowest ERA's still fight the jitters before taking the mound.

Perhaps it's a little more pronounced in fundraising, simply because nothing in the way most of us were raised has prepared us for asking for money.

From the anxiety we felt as children asking our

parents for a dollar or two, to the discomfort we've all experienced when pressed for a loan by friends or relatives in a pinch, we find such transactions innately unsettling.

Further, many of us were raised to believe it's a sign of weakness to have to ask – and we still harbor this feeling when we set about soliciting gifts.

Perhaps the problem is this: we see ourselves begging for money for a needy cause rather than offering others an opportunity to invest in an organization that's addressing important needs in the community.

But offering a life-enhancing opportunity is precisely what we're doing, and it's essential to adopt this perspective. It's not begging when a donor's gift provides housing for the homeless, food for the hungry, scholarships for deserving students, or medical help for those suffering from chronic conditions.

It's not begging when the organization, on whose behalf you're asking, is stable, accountable, and successful in its work. By no means is it begging; it is an investment you seek.

In all the years I've asked for money, I still get butterflies before making a call. Once I'm into it, particularly if I'm with another board or staff member, that discomfort fades. But it comes right back before my next call.

So expect the flutters. Welcome them as a reminder of how important this visit is. Just don't let them weaken your resolve.

17

MISTAKE

The state of the economy is key to fundraising

During the calamitous recession of 2008 – our greatest financial upheaval since the Great Depression - giving dipped only by two percent (five percent when adjusted for inflation). Despite the cutbacks, layoffs, and family belt-tightening, over $500 billion was still contributed to charitable organizations in America.

So even when times are bad, we shouldn't second-guess whether someone will give.

The late Hank Rosso, great teacher of philanthropy and mentor to many, said we should never deny anyone the right to say no ... or yes.

He was right.

The stock market could be sagging, earnings soft, inventories swelling, but still you ask. Why? For two reasons:

1) You can't really make valid assumptions about another's financial situation, and

2) Individuals may be more embarrassed by not being asked (when they learn their friends and colleagues have been) than by having to say no or give a smaller gift.

If people care deeply about an issue, they'll often find a way to support it. Maybe not at the level you had hoped, but frequently they'll come through.

Recently, I made a gift that was a big stretch for me. But the arts organization with which I've been involved for 20 years made such a compelling case for the timeliness of the investment that I found a way. And I'm typical of many others.

When deciding whether to give, a donor considers a range of factors. Among them are: the integrity of the organization, her link to it, the passion she feels for the cause, the "return" she's received on a previous investment, and the ability of the asker to convey the urgency of giving now.

Certainly the state of the economy and the investments in a personal portfolio influence the decision to give. But by no means do they dictate it.

18

MISTAKE

Wealth is what mostly determines a person's willingness to give

When an individual makes a philanthropic gift, at least three factors come into play. He or she has:

• A connection to the organization

• Concern for the cause

• The financial capacity to give

Common sense tells you that the first two far outweigh the third. A person can have incalculable wealth, but if she's not connected to the people or services of your organization or doesn't display interest in what you're doing, she's not likely to give.

I know of one organization that wined and dined a man with huge financial resources, hoping for a lead gift. He had a known interest in the kind of work the group did, and he had assets.

But he didn't have a connection to the organization nor – and this is key – a habit of giving. In fact, no one could recall him ever making a significant gift, though countless organizations had cultivated him. After months of negotiations the wooing came to an end. "No dice," the man finally said. Psychologically, he couldn't let loose of the money.

Time was wasted and, even worse, the person who ultimately did step forward with the lead gift felt ignored during the process.

I probably see this mistake more than any other. Someone will excitedly hand me a list – of potential donors, of people to interview for a feasibility study, of individuals to invite to a particular function. When I ask how these folks are connected to the organization, more often than not the answer is "they aren't – but they have money."

Too often, as a starting point, board and staff members will scribble down the names of wealthy people in the community. Give that up. Instead, list only the people you know who share your organization's values. Not only will they be more responsive, they'll also be willing to link you to others (perhaps with more money) who care about what you do.

19

MISTAKE

To secure a gift, saying just the right words is key

If this were true, we could all carry the same script when calling upon prospects and be done with it. We could all use the same foundation or corporation proposals. And all fundraising letters would be nearly identical.

While there are certain things you should say and do because we know they work – using inclusive language comes to mind, "Join with us," "Be part of" or "I know from our conversations that you and I share a belief in..." – even these can be set aside if you have a better way of saying the same thing and getting the right result.

The only "right words" are those that reflect you and the organization, and those you know are "right" for the donor because you've been a good listener and discerned what she cares about.

Are there formulas? Of course. In direct mail the simplest one I know is: touch my heart, tell me what the problem is, tell me what you're doing about it, and tell me how I can help. But those aren't the words – that is the framework.

Grant proposals also have a structure that should be followed, usually provided by the potential funder. But the way you fill in the blanks with your passion and programs is critical.

As for what to say when calling upon a prospective donor, that depends on the two of you. Remember, you're having a conversation – it has to feel natural.

The best advice is perhaps the simplest – be yourself. Oh sure, you'll want to remember what you learned in your training sessions. For example, try to avoid such phrases as "Anything you can give will be great," or "I'm sorry to be bothering you...." But what's most important is to say what feels most comfortable. And accept that the words won't flow perfectly.

One volunteer, intimidated by a prospect she was calling on who was older and in a higher position in the same company, finally asked the man for the gift – $25,000. He seemed stunned, and said no one had ever asked him for a gift that size. She blurted out the first thing that came to her mind: "Well, I've never ASKED anyone for a gift that size." They both laughed ... and he made the gift.

20

MISTAKE

You don't have to give money yourself – your gift is your time

This mistaken belief continues to plague board leaders and development officers as they work to ensure that *every* member of the board makes an annual gift or a pledge to the campaign.

For generations, there was perhaps a belief on the part of many board members and volunteers that time and money were interchangeable. But that day is long past.

Now donors – individuals as well as foundations and corporations – routinely ask about the level of board support. Some even want to know what percentage of the board has contributed (the current expectation is 100 percent) and what the aggregate giving is. To respond that your board gives its time no longer satisfies.

But there's another key reason why you have to reach into your own pocket: you can't effectively ask for a gift until you've given yourself. A funny thing happens when you write out your own check. Not only does it feel good, it deepens your commitment to the cause. Suddenly you become a vocal advocate and want everyone else to feel as good. Your enthusiasm becomes contagious.

And don't forget that donors are wise. They'll often question you about your own support. If you, who are closest to the organization, haven't made a financial commitment, your appeal to them is an empty one. "Come back when you've decided what you're going to give," they'll sometimes say.

As a board member, you should expect to be asked for an annual or capital gift (or better yet, both) in a personal meeting with the board chair and CEO. Only then – in the context of your service being acknowledged and your ongoing role in the organization discussed – will the request for your gift be like the one you'll eventually make of others.

You, too, deserve to experience the joy of giving.

21

MISTAKE

It's impolite to ask for a specific amount

It troubles many people to ask for a specified amount. They believe it reveals to the donor that the organization has gathered lots of personal information about him (net worth, real estate holdings, giving history, gifts to other organizations). They also balk at putting the number out there, fearing it'll cause surprise, resentment, or anger.

But step aside for a moment, and look at it from the donor's perspective. If you've approached things right, the person you're calling upon is acquainted with your organization, knows the purpose of your visit, and has agreed to meet with you.

Probably the biggest unknown, as far as the donor is concerned, is just how much you're seeking.

I've been on calls when someone on our team will

(regrettably) say, "And so, Charlie, we hope you'll consider being part of this effort to build a community theater and that you'll make a significant gift." Significant gift. What does that mean? $5,000? $50,000? $500,000?

You need to cite a specific amount – or, if not an exact amount, at least a range.

Most capital campaigns (and many annual campaigns too) use either a gift range chart or a list of naming opportunities ("For a gift of $1 million, this facility will bear the name of your loved one").

Some askers, uncomfortable with citing a figure, will hand the chart to the prospect. "We were hoping you'd consider making a leadership gift in the range of $10,000 to $25,000. Is that something you'll consider?" Not as good as asking for $25,000 outright, but better than being completely vague.

Be as specific as you can with your request. Rather than be resentful, your prospect will likely respect that you've done your homework.

22

MISTAKE

Asking once a year is enough

Decades ago, when I was first involved in Stanford University fundraising as a volunteer, I served on what was called the Creative Committee. We were a group of alums with a background in marketing and fundraising who advised the annual fund office.

I remember how we prided ourselves on our fall campaign letter – usually signed by the university president – promising that if an alum gave when the letter was received (usually in September), he wouldn't hear from us or be "bothered again" until the following September.

I shudder to remember that. It conveyed, first, that asking and giving were a "bother," and second that we only cared to contact the alum when we wanted money.

Fortunately, this is long in Stanford's past. But I see the practice repeated in organizations that are newer to fundraising. Because we believe people feel put upon when asked, we want to keep the irritation as low as possible.

What we fail to understand is the joy our donors feel when giving, all the more enhanced when we can show the impact of their past and current gifts.

Even though a donor's gift may have been recent, we can still let her know that as successful as our tutoring program is, we've identified 40 more eligible students who are now on a waiting list. Is this something she'd be willing to help us with?

Over the years, one of the benefits I've found in engaging volunteers in thankathons (see Mistake #36) is the power of hearing a donor say how much it means to be able to give. It turns out that giving isn't a bother at all.

Ask because you're succeeding, not because you need money. And ask more than once because the need is growing ... as is your impact on the community.

23

MISTAKE

Development staff, because it's their job, are more effective in asking

Although many universities and other larger institutions have converted to staff-only fundraising, it's a mistake in my view.

While development staff may be more "effective" from the standpoint of being thoroughly trained in asking, and having at their disposal a reservoir of facts and information about the organization, still these advantages pale in comparison to what you offer.

First, as a board member, you bring a particular passion and perspective to the table based on your decision to become involved. It is not your job. You don't have to show up. But you do. And your voluntary involvement lends great credibility to the organization you represent.

Second, fundraising isn't about personal eloquence or asking in a perfect way. It's about relationships and respect and influence. It is the rare staff person who travels in the same social circles as his prospective donors.

Finally, in the mind of the would-be donor, a development officer is paid to ask. In fact, his livelihood is tied up with getting a "yes." You on the other hand are in the irreproachable position of having nothing to gain from your visit except the satisfaction of furthering a cause you believe in.

You are every bit as effective in asking as the development officer. And, as a team, the two of you are all but unstoppable.

And speaking of teamwork, there's sometimes a mistaken notion that with a good development director, the board can be less involved in fundraising.

In fact the opposite is true. With a skilled development director, expect to be more engaged in fundraising.

I've heard board members say – often at the beginning of a search process – that they can hardly wait to hire a development director so they can get some rest from all the fundraising.

I quickly counsel that any professional worth her salt will expect (and implicitly demand) a board that's fully committed to donor relations and fundraising.

Great development directors are choreographers,

conductors, and facilitators. They provide structure, offer training, develop materials, give direction, and often accompany board members on certain calls.

A development director is a partner, one who assigns, prods, cajoles, cheerleads, and keeps things organized. But he or she cannot succeed without you and your wholehearted commitment.

24

MISTAKE

Fundraising consultants (and development officers) often bring with them a list of people to solicit

A colleague of mine, who had worked at a major hospital during its capital campaign, was recently hired by another organization.

When she arrived on the job, the board and CEO said, "Well, where's the list?" My friend was incredulous. At first, she thought they were kidding. But, they were unrelenting that she hand over the list of people who had contributed to the hospital's campaign. After a few months, she resigned.

Carrying a list of prospects from one organization to another is a breach of fundraising ethics. Why? Because the individuals on the list have relationships with the organization that have been developed over time.

Traveling lists would be a practice that treats donors like a commodity instead of as investors motivated by mission and shared values.

Are there exceptions to the rule? No. But there are acceptable practices that can draw on a consultant's knowledge.

For example, if in your database there's a prospect being actively cultivated, and it's someone with whom the consultant has worked with in another organization, it is perfectly ethical for her to offer insights, comments, and strategies based on her knowledge of the person.

It is also within the ethical code for a consultant, in reviewing your lists of potential prospects, to comment on her experience with someone on the lists.

But don't expect consultants or new staff to bring a list with them from another organization: your own ethics will be called into question.

25

MISTAKE

We can run this campaign on the cheap

One of my early lessons in fund development was that you have to spend money to raise money. Yet, so many organizations still struggle with this reality.

Board members and CFOs often try to stint on both "soft" and "hard" costs.

One such board, preparing for a several hundred million dollar campaign, asked their CFO to challenge a relatively small expense I (the consultant) had recommended for "cultivation." The money was to cover a tour of the facility followed by an informal lunch gathering, as well as a pair of receptions for long-time donors.

Only after I went through a lengthy explanation of why people had to be cultivated before they could be asked for six and seven-figure gifts did the CFO recommend that the board back down.

Another so-called soft item that's often neglected is training. I've known boards to limp along in their solicitations because they refused to hire a trainer to help them learn effective ways to state the case, rescue a solicitation that's not going well, and handle objections.

But hard items such as materials and personnel aren't spared either. I've seen campaign brochures so amateurish they lacked all credibility. I've also come into organizations where development staffing levels were so bare bones people were fatigued, angry, and devoid of any motivation.

Clearly, you must contain the costs of fundraising – this isn't the place for extravagance. But penny-pinching a campaign's infrastructure will eventually backfire.

You'd be smarter to delay your campaign than to starve it.

26

MISTAKE

Fundraising costs are a measure of our organization

One of the best lessons I ever learned was from a savvy VP for Finance who taught me about "break points" – points beyond which you need to add staff or other resources if the spirit of those trying to raise money isn't to be broken.

While it's important to be able to say your fundraising costs are low (e.g. 15 cents of every dollar), that may not always be a good thing. There are times when you *need* to spend more. Otherwise, you can't compete for big dollars in the wider marketplace.

For example, I worked with a public media outlet that resisted adding staff and updating its software to track donors. The board didn't want to "spend all that money." Results: the organization missed a sizable funding opportunity (there was no one to write the foundation proposal); their major giving program took a back seat to the demands of direct mail; the development director quit; and the reputation of the organization among development professionals was so poor no one with qualifications applied. The organization limped along for nearly a year without leadership and it took years to recover.

We do no service to anyone when we underpay and overwork our staff and refuse to retain the help and expertise they periodically need. High turnover, lack of motivation, obsolete hardware and software – all are chronic problems in our sector.

Those organizations we admire are often the ones that make a sufficient investment to keep good people and systems. Even those agencies with a full complement of volunteers willing to fundraise need competent staff to help them succeed.

In a start-up, or at the beginning of a capital campaign, an organization may spend as much as 40 cents on the dollar to raise money. As the organization matures (and as the campaign succeeds), the cost per dollar raised will decline dramatically.

By all means, let it be known how prudent you are with your dollars. But make it just as clear that you're willing to invest in building relationships, and that entails costs for marketing, stewardship, public relations, as well as fundraising. Those values are as respected as the values that undergird your programs.

27

MISTAKE

You need a powerful board to have a successful campaign

There are organizations across America – particularly universities, hospitals and large arts and cultural organizations – whose boards are the envy of all.

The people on these boards are leaders in commerce, industry, education, and possess wealth and connections in abundance.

Annually they provide leadership gifts of six and even seven figures. And during a capital campaign, their gifts often constitute as much as 80 percent of the total goal.

If this doesn't sound like your board, well, join the crowd. For every organization so blessed, there are thousands upon thousands with boards more like yours.

These organizations are governed by people who care deeply about the mission, bring what wealth and connections they have, and are willing to work to fulfill the vision. And they excel.

Even if yours isn't a "power" board, you can still have a successful campaign. Probably the most common solution is to form a campaign cabinet or steering committee that engages several members of the board as well as high-profile leaders in the community.

I've found that while many "movers and shakers" may not want to join the board, or be involved on an ongoing basis, they will participate in a time-limited campaign, assuming they have some passion for the project.

A food bank I know of used this model for its capital campaign and surpassed its goal. Religious organizations have for years used the same approach with great success. And social service organizations often form campaign leadership organizations that involve both board and non-board volunteers.

Power is a relative concept. Enlist the right people, even if they're not on your board, and suddenly your organization too has the power to mount a successful campaign.

28

MISTAKE

Not everyone on the board has to be involved in fundraising

"Not me. I'm dreadful at it."

"You can't be serious. I couldn't peddle cheese to a mouse."

"All things equal, I prefer the guillotine."

Maybe that's how YOU feel about asking for money, but that doesn't mean you're off the hook. Still, you'll probably like what I'm about to say.

Everyone on the board must be involved in raising money, but not everyone has to ASK. Leaving the asking to a committee is frequently done; but no sensible organization leaves board members out of the full "development" process.

Let me clarify. There is a difference between "development" and fundraising.

Development is the process of identifying and cultivating potential donors, and maintaining relationships once these individuals have given. Fundraising focuses on the actual asking.

It is the responsibility of the entire board to be involved in development, while it's possible that only selected members involve themselves in asking.

One board member I worked with insisted she would "do anything but ask for money," a common refrain. I asked how she'd like to help. "Well, I know lots of people," she informed me, "and I have good lists."

This was indeed the case.

We used her lists extensively when we held our cultivation events. And, when all was said and done, nearly a quarter of all the money raised was from donors she directed us to.

While you don't necessarily have to ask for a gift yourself, you do have to accept responsibility for assisting in the most productive way you can.

29

MISTAKE

It's prudent to focus
on large donors only

Anyone who contributes to your cause is interested in it and has the potential to become more involved, whether by giving again or participating in another way.

Ironically, by focusing only on those who give large gifts, you jeopardize your fiscal health in years to come. Remember, giving is cyclical. Those who contribute smaller amounts in their 30's may become your major donors in their 40's or 50's. And these very same small givers will in all probability be your legacy donors in their later years.

When you ignore smaller donors, you lose sight of the following:

1) Anyone, no matter the size of his gift, can become a champion for you. Astute organizations understand this. Especially during economic downturns, they keep

donors engaged – through increased communication, invitations to recognition and outreach events, and involvement as volunteers. These organizations recognize that the gift alone doesn't always mirror the donor's real commitment to you.

2) Giving according to one's means should be respected. What about the donor for whom a gift of $100 represents a greater share of income than another's gift of $1,000? Do we minimize the gift and dishonor her commitment?

As our society ages, more and more people are on fixed incomes. They deserve our outreach, not only for the obvious potential of estate gifts, but also because many are alone and our contact gives them joy. Let us not lose sight of the historic meaning of the word philanthropy, "love of people."

3) Many a donor dips his toe in the water first. Often a donor will test an organization with a small gift, withholding a larger sum until he sees how his small gift is acknowledged, what use it is put to, and what further overtures will be made.

Reach as deeply into your donor base as you can with your gratitude. Not only will you communicate a great deal about your organization's values, you'll create legions of new champions as well.

30

MISTAKE

Estate gifts only come from big donors

If there's one mistake that's being challenged daily, it is this one. We read all the time about the $25 donor who bequeaths $1 million to the local animal shelter, or the decades-lapsed donor whose estate provides hundreds of thousands of dollars to an organization in which she or her husband was once active.

Recently, you may have heard about the homeless man in Phoenix who left an estate of $4 million – including charitable gifts of $400,000 to several institutions. National Public Radio was one.

In his will, he asked that these words be said when his gift was acknowledged as helping to support NPR: "Support for NPR comes from the estate of Richard Leroy Walters, whose life was enriched by NPR and whose bequest seeks to encourage others to discover public radio."

More and more organizations are getting smart about estate gifts. They're looking to members and other volunteers as well as steady donors of $100 or less, and educating them about the possibility of simple bequests and other deferred giving options.

One nonprofit I know worked with a loyal volunteer, a retired schoolteacher, to help her see how her estate could benefit the organization. She put her modest house in a trust. When she died years later, the property values in her community had soared. Her house, for which she paid $10,000, commanded nearly a million dollars. Yet, this woman's annual gift had never exceeded $100.

Why did she do it? Because whenever she thought of the future of this children's services agency – where she had volunteered for 40 years – she wanted to be part of it. Her legacy – invested prudently and supporting programs in perpetuity – ensures that she is.

31

You need a stable of annual donors to have a successful capital campaign

Certainly, it's easier to have a capital campaign if you have a large group of annual donors. But don't make the mistake of thinking you absolutely need them to raise capital dollars. Organizations with relatively small annual giving programs have been successful at capital campaigns.

For example, the food bank I mentioned earlier had a limited number of annual donors. But because of the organization's visibility, the growing evidence that better food distribution was needed, and because of its reputation for solid management, the group was able to convince would-be donors that a new facility was needed. People invested at high levels.

Start-up organizations often seek capital funding

long before they have a base of annual donors. An independent high school in Southern California raised $34 million for the initial phase of its buildings – two years before the school enrolled its first student or started an annual fund. The promise was great, the values were clear, and the community rallied to help create this new opportunity for its young people.

Then, too, there's the success of a domestic violence policy organization I'm familiar with. When the group launched its capital and endowment campaigns, there were few annual donors. Despite this, the agency is very close now to both its endowment and capital goals. And the gifts range from $25 to $7.5 million – most from people who'd never given before.

It's important to build a strong annual giving program – for lots of reasons. But, if you've never attracted many annual donors or are just starting out, don't be discouraged.

With a bold vision, a compelling case, a recognized and valid community need, a committed inner corps, and a solid plan, you can raise the money you need.

32

MISTAKE

If you don't know how much a prospect can give, shoot for the moon

In a way it's flattering to be asked for a large gift, even when we can't afford it (we all like to appear prosperous, it seems). But that doesn't mean you should ask for an unsupportable amount.

Vastly overreaching a person's capacity makes you look foolish and creates doubts about your organization's credibility.

If a donor has never given you more than $1,000 and her largest capital gift to any cause was $25,000, you will err – and perhaps embarrass or rankle her – by asking for $100,000 unless there's some recent circumstance (inheritance, for instance) that has changed her capacity to give.

But let me quickly add a cautionary note: don't ask

for too little either. If someone has a philanthropic pattern of giving at a certain level, don't lowball your request because of certain assumptions ("That new sunroom cost plenty" or "I know you just helped your daughter with a down payment on her house"). You'll get the low amount. Quickly.

Instead, strike the right amount based on research and first-hand knowledge of the person's wealth and giving potential.

I remember when, as a leadership volunteer, I was asked by the campaign chair for a gift of $20,000. I was stunned. At the time I had children in college and my income was fairly modest. I had planned to give $10,000 ($2,000 per year for 5 years). However, I was honestly flattered that I was viewed as capable of making such a gift. I thought about my feelings towards the institution and my own leadership role in the campaign. I ended up giving $15,000 over 5 years – and it felt good.

Stretch is good – pie in the sky asking is not.

33

MISTAKE

Some can't afford to give and shouldn't even be asked

I have sat at boardroom tables for years, reviewing lists with board members, and over and over I hear:

- "Oh, they can't give. They don't have any money."
- "Them? They're paying off a pledge to their museum – they won't be able to give." Or,
- "Their daughter's wedding is next month. They've got to be tapped out."

But second-guessing whether someone can give only invites problems. You risk offending the donor (who may in fact want to be asked) and miss the opportunity of connecting the person with your organization even if she can't give right now.

Years ago, when I was the volunteer chair for an educational fundraising effort, my steering committee and I hit the fourth year of a five-year campaign and, in truth, we were exhausted.

We debated whether to continue soliciting in a very personal way, or to surrender some prospects to a more generic approach. We even discussed whether it was necessary to call upon everyone if we reached our goal beforehand.

One of our steering committee members told a story that inspired us to soldier on. In her home city, there was a recent dedication of a new cultural center. With her husband away, she invited a friend to accompany her. The friend hesitated and said she wasn't interested. Sensing a problem, our committee member gently probed. It turns out the women was resentful because no one had ever asked her for a gift to the new center, and she felt their campaign leadership had made an assumption she couldn't give.

This sobering story helped us stay the course, exceed our goal, and cover more than 90 percent of our assigned prospects.

Never assume someone can't give.

34

MISTAKE

You need a feasibility study before launching a capital campaign

A feasibility study, in which board and community representatives are queried about an organization's image, its visibility in the community, its proposed campaign, and the likelihood of the interviewee contributing, used to be standard preparation for a capital or endowment drive. Today, more and more organizations are going forward without such a study.

The reasons vary. Some groups understand full well that no matter what the study shows, they must proceed anyway. The school has to be expanded. The roof needs to be replaced. The birthing unit must be built.

Other agencies, having delayed their campaign due to a previous study's recommendation, feel they have enough information now to go forward.

Still other organizations consider the cost of a study, usually between $15,000 and $50,000, prohibitive, and are convinced they'll succeed without one.

Lastly, a growing number of agencies are identifying leadership gifts in the earliest planning stages of their campaign, thereby removing one of the key purposes of a feasibility study. They're talking directly to the prospects, getting their buy-in on the campaign from the very beginning. And they're making their decision to move forward based on the promise of these gifts.

Don't get me wrong. I'm not against feasibility studies. I've conducted scores of them myself. They serve to get your case out into the community, reveal perceptions about your organization, and gauge in a confidential setting the interviewee's interest in giving or volunteering. In other words, there are definite benefits to a feasibility study.

Still, it would be a mistake to think your success hinges on one.

35

If you've been trained in asking at one organization, you needn't attend another agency's training

While the training at the natural history museum may have been stellar, and although many of the principles will transfer to the youth symphony, you still need to be trained in how to ask for the youth symphony.

When I conduct a board training or coaching session, I often hear that certain people aren't attending because they already know how to ask. That may be true – they may be skilled solicitors – but there are things particular to each organization that affect how you ask.

You are vulnerable to a great deal of discomfort if you don't get organization-specific training.

For example, you need 'Talking Points,' a list of the

compelling reasons why the organization merits support. You need to hear what the common objections are and how to respond to them.

You need stories and statistics you can use to inform your prospects, as well as information about budgets, the cost of fundraising, and how your endowment (if any) is managed.

Then too, you'll get your best practice in asking for this particular organization, using a script.

If all that isn't enough, one last advantage of attending the training is to get to know your fellow solicitors better. You just might identify the right person to team up with to make your calls considerably more comfortable ... and effective.

As I've said elsewhere in this book, the most important thing in any solicitation is to be yourself, to converse naturally. But that doesn't mean flying by the seat of your pants. Good training builds confidence.

36

MISTAKE

For those giving small gifts, a simple acknowledgment is fitting

If this isn't the biggest mistake I'll cite in these pages, it's a close runner-up.

When deciding which donors to focus on, size does matter for most organizations. The more a donor gives, the more an organization invests in him with perks, tangible gifts, and appreciation lunches. And it would be a mistake not to continue to nurture your biggest investors.

But we're out of balance with the nature of philanthropy when we neglect lower level donors and offer only perfunctory thanks. Equally bad is our failure to evaluate these donors for their future giving potential (with the result that great donors often languish in the 'auto-receipt' pile).

What a missed opportunity.

At any level, people should be thanked personally for their gifts. One effective way is to organize a quarterly or biannual 'Thankathon," during which board and volunteers call every donor (yes, every donor) and thank them.

This can be a highly productive event for several reasons:

1) Thankathons tangibly show donors how much you value them. Not many organizations take the trouble to make these calls. That yours does will be remembered by the donor.

2) Thankatons can tell you a great deal about your supporters. Often donors are forthcoming about why they're giving, what initially piqued their interest, and may even offer constructive feedback about your organization.

3) Thankathons can quell a volunteer's fears about asking. Donors will often express how happy they are to give. When a caller hears this, it validates that people do like to give. Participating in a thankathon is often the first step towards a caller agreeing to solicit others.

Whether you thank with a printed card, a phone call, or a formal note, remember this is just the beginning. Stay connected. It's the only way to build a relationship with the donor and earn his loyalty and lasting support.

37

MISTAKE

If someone is already contributing to an organization similar to yours, asking her to give to you is poaching

Recently I had breakfast with a friend who complained that "I gave to the whales and now I'm hearing from the dolphins, gorillas and pandas!" When I asked if he was giving to these other organizations, he said: "Of course I am. I love animals."

Always keep in mind that philanthropy is driven by issues and values, not by organizations and their needs.

If a person cares deeply about music in the schools, for example, and is already giving to an organization with this as its mission, she is in fact the most likely prospect to give to another organization with the same goal. It is not an either/or, it is a both/and.

While institutional loyalty (a person's college, prep school, place of worship) still commands part of a person's philanthropy, we see increasingly that people invest in similar organizations because they want a particular need fulfilled.

Those who support one environmental organization gravitate toward others; people supporting one museum invariably contribute to others in the community; those drawn to cancer research or homeless issues are known to support multiple organizations with related purposes.

From time to time, you'll be shown newsletters or annual reports or special events programs listing the names of donors (or, better yet, you'll be on the lookout yourself for such lists). You'll be asked if you know any of these people or have a connection to them.

If you worry about "poaching" these donors from other groups, don't think you have the power. The person you approach decides for himself where to direct his philanthropy.

If you like, encourage him to support your cause in addition to others. But in the end, it's his decision not yours. All you're doing is presenting the opportunity.

38

MISTAKE

Your goal in a major gifts or capital campaign is simply the amount of money you need

Success in a capital or endowment campaign shouldn't be measured in dollars alone.

There are four purposes for any sizable campaign: raise the money, raise the organization's visibility, increase the pool of donors, and move the organization to the next level of performance.

Raising the money is clearly the primary purpose. Every person involved must be committed to, and willing to work toward, achieving the financial goal.

Raising visibility is a second aim. A successful campaign allows you to disseminate your message widely and reach potential supporters who currently aren't on your radar screen.

Engaging more donors is a third goal of a large campaign, as these intensive bursts tend to be inclusive of all types and sizes of donors. In any major campaign, you'll find yourself supported by friends of friends, by a board member's next-door neighbor, or the granddaughter of an early benefactor. All of these people could prove invaluable in the future as volunteers, donors, or champions.

Finally, taking the organization to the next level of excellence is the ultimate objective of any campaign. It is, after all, the reason you're raising money in the first place. From this point forward, your hospital will serve a broader community more capably, your school's endowment will ensure a higher level of diversity through scholarship support, your homeless shelter will accommodate families as well as single women, or your orchestra will be assured because its endowed chairs will attract the very best musicians.

Campaigns are hard work. No doubt about it. But strangely enough, when you understand the other ramifications of a campaign, raising the money becomes just a bit easier.

39

MISTAKE

Consultants aren't needed if you have a fundraising staff

Too often, board members hesitate to hire a consultant, believing staff can do everything. But as with any business, there are times when a consultant's perspective is not only useful, it's required.

There are at least three jobs that call for the objective perspective and special expertise of a consultant. They are:

1. *Campaign Feasibility Study.* If you choose to do one, it must be conducted by an outsider if the results are to be credible. These one-on-one interviews with board members and others who represent the community are more candid and confidential if undertaken by someone unaffiliated with the organization.

2. *Strategic Planning.* Whether for the development department or for the entire organization, overseeing this

often lengthy process is best left to an outsider – someone free to challenge, stretch, and ignite the thinking of the board and staff.

For one thing – and it's key – staff will be more candid about their aspirations as well as the constraints upon them. And, the time it takes to formulate a strategic plan is too distracting for a staff person with a full workload already.

3. *Development Audit.* This unbiased review of your fundraising practices and performance is an important periodic checkup for improving and adjusting the ways in which you raise money.

Because of a vested interest in their job, and strategies and materials in which they've played a prominent role, staff can't be expected to conduct an objective audit.

When staff requests approval for a consultant, there are usually legitimate reasons. Listen to them. Not only will a consultant relieve internal pressure, he or she can provide an external, objective perspective on the next best step for your organization to take.

40

MISTAKE

Nowadays, people want you to get to the point and ask – cultivation wastes time

This mistake is sometimes made by those on the board who don't want cultivation themselves – they're ready to give, impatient to be asked, and don't want to waste time in what they sometimes call "the dance."

Often these are young people, with new wealth. And chances are they've done their own research on the potential donors they want to approach.

Or, they may be "old school" fundraising volunteers – ones steeped in the tradition of philanthropy. They have all served on boards and, owing to a sense of noblesse oblige, routinely support each other's causes.

But, excepting these two very specific types, it's a good practice to assume that people want to be cultivated. They want to get to know you, understand what your organization is about, and learn how they can be involved.

If you approach them prematurely, they'll often turn you down or give much less than you hoped for. They may not have had time to become fully comfortable with your organization. Perhaps they haven't had a chance to interact with the executive director. Or they're not yet convinced of the urgency of your mission.

Having said that, it's important to understand that philanthropy must be flexible enough to accommodate the differing styles of donors drawn to the promise of doing something meaningful in their communities.

While it's safe to assume people still want what has been called the "institutional hug," don't press your style on them. Find out what they need in terms of cultivation. Talk to staff. Talk to their friends. Best of all, engage the potential donor and listen to what he himself desires. "I'm glad we've had this tour. As you think about what you've seen, what are your questions? Are there other programs you'd like to see?"

The two ears to one mouth ratio is a magic anatomical reality. Use it when determining the amount and type of cultivation to offer.

41

MISTAKE

If your early fundraising calls don't spark interest, chances are your cause isn't important enough

It's easy to get discouraged at the outset of a campaign if the leadership gifts you planned on don't materialize. This is especially true when you've laid out a solid strategy and if the people who declined were the very ones that seemed excited and indicated they'd be willing to give.

When this happens, you need to step back from the sting of rejection and take a hard look at the prospects you've called on. How might you have been successful with them – and how can you have a better chance with the leading prospects that remain.

It may have been the way you asked, or who asked.

Or it could have been a circumstance having nothing to do with you (an illness, an unforeseen expense, a drop in corporate revenues).

As a first step, go back and ask those who turned you down to tell you why ... honestly. A "no" isn't always a "no" – sometimes it's a "Not now." Sometimes it's a "No, not for that amount." But you don't know until you ask.

I remember, a few years back, when a donor who had pledged more than $2 million backed away from his commitment because of a plunge in net worth. It was a huge blow to the campaign.

Needless to say, the organization was discouraged but it didn't give up.

Several board members reviewed various options with the donor and he eventually agreed to pay quarterly installments over several years. This worked for the donor, who felt his assets would recover during the period of the payments. And it worked for the organization: it kept the campaign alive, and gave them vital cash flow for their work.

Once you know why your first attempts failed, there are three questions to wrestle with:

• "Will it make a difference to the community if we abandon this program or project?" If no, then it's doubtful your campaign was merited in the first place. You're probably right to give it up.

• "Have we made the case in a compelling way – is it

urgent, relevant, and exciting to the community?" If no, then you need to sharpen your message, perhaps using feedback from those who initially rejected you.

Years ago, I consulted with a fraternal organization attempting to raise money for a new headquarters building. After a few initial gifts, the campaign stalled.

To learn why, I spoke with several of the prospects who had refused to give. It turned out they weren't interested in the building campaign but did fully back the organization's leadership development and scholarship programs. They were eager to give to those.

We were able to refocus the campaign and reposition the case. It was a huge success, and we used other unrestricted monies to complete the headquarters.

• "Do we have other lead prospects we can approach, with the goal of engaging them to bring others into the campaign?" If no, then you might postpone your campaign in favor of identifying and cultivating other potential supporters.

Unless there's hard evidence that your campaign is ill-conceived, giving up on it should be a last resort.

42

We can probably count on a few "windfall" gifts

The operative word in this mistake is "count on." Early in my career a wise counselor once told me, "Don't expect a miracle, but be ready for it."

We hear about windfall gifts because, like casino winnings, they're the exception. People like to talk about them. Soon they become legendary. My life has been peppered with such stories. The woman who walked into the homeless shelter with a $25,000 check in hand. The church that found $30,000 in the collection plate with a note, "I thought it was time I did something for the restoration campaign." The cathedral that received notice of a $1 million estate gift from the surviving partner of a parishioner who died many years before – the gift topped off their capital campaign.

In truth, there are usually a few surprise gifts in most

campaigns. They frequently come towards the end – from someone who's been monitoring your progress with interest and wants to be part of your success.

But don't expect any godsends, and don't inflate your revenue projections. Doing so will subject you to unrealistic expectations, and your inability to meet them will degrade people's confidence in your projections.

Instead, you have to plan for every single gift. Compiling lists of potential donors, determining how much they can give, educating them about the organization and drawing them closer to it – these are the underpinnings of successful fundraising.

Yes, someone has to win the lottery, as you often hear. Just don't bank on it being you.

43

MISTAKE

Fundraising is a lot easier once you get the hang of it

In some ways, the very act of asking does get easier after a while. You learn what to say, how to handle objections, how to keep the conversation flowing, how to phrase your request for a gift.

But even though asking may become easier, fundraising remains a daunting task on two levels.

On a personal level, you continually must deal with your own reservations, the ever real possibility of embarrassment, and whatever fears you have about rejection. And in spite of years of practice, these concerns may lessen but never subside.

But fundraising is also daunting on a second, broader level because of what's at stake – namely, your organization and the people who depend on you, sometimes for their very health and well-being. As a result, every solicitation has to be as right as you can make it.

Personally, when I'm asked to make a call as a volunteer, it helps me to keep in mind that if I don't succeed, a little girl whom I can picture won't have the special ed care she needs, or an aging citizen in my community will be forced to move from his home to an institution. That way, it's no longer about me. Or even about the organization. It's about the people who will benefit. We are not the end users of the gifts we raise. Remember that.

You'll encounter those who claim to love asking and display little hesitation. Perhaps this even describes you. But even here a word of caution is needed.

Never approach fundraising casually. Your success hinges on your knowing as much as possible about your prospective donor – his interests, passions, and needs. That takes time.

Further, you need to be knowledgeable enough about your cause to answer hard questions. Undoubtedly you'll get them.

So if you're getting the hang of asking, savor the feeling. But remember, seasoned professionals look upon each solicitation with a bit of fear and a lot of respect. As volunteers, we should do the same.

44

MISTAKE

With so many causes raising money, the wells of philanthropy are drying up

This in my opinion is a "crutch" mistake – one that says "We didn't succeed because of the competition in our community."

People give according to the things they value and want to see continued in their communities: education, religion, arts, culture, environmental causes. And as long as the organizations they support meet these needs with effective and fiscally sound programs, they will continue to give.

In fact, philanthropy has grown exponentially over the years, following suit with the burgeoning number of nonprofits in the U.S. (now estimated to be more than 1.5 million).

Before declaring the well has run dry – and forsaking the people who rely on you – make sure the dipping bucket is working right. Perhaps you haven't lowered it deep enough to reach the next level of water.

Review the results of your various fundraising efforts. How successful are your events? Mailings? What outreach have you made to donors? Have you marketed the impact of what you're doing? Are you staffed adequately to compete in a crowded marketplace? Are there opportunities for collaboration with similar organizations?

In all likelihood doubts about the wells of philanthropy running dry are simply doubts about your organization's ability to do what's necessary to raise money in today's competitive and chaotic climate.

Because of the importance we play in the well-being and enrichment of our communities, we cannot let excuses stand in the way of our outreach. The wells have not run dry. Nor will they. It is our ability to innovate and inspire that must be replenished.

A Final Word

"Mistakes are painful when they happen, but years later a collection of mistakes is what is called experience."

–Denis Waitley

This book reflects my experience. These are mistakes I have observed. They are also mistakes I have made.

In working with hundreds of boards and thousands of board members over the years, I have seen all of these and more.

But I have also witnessed the triumph of overcoming these mistakes, and I savor memories of excited calls from those I have coached.

I recall the board member who persuaded her CEO that, yes, they could ask for $1 million from a certain couple, even though others on the board had decided "they probably don't have that kind of money." It literally took less than a minute for the couple to say "yes."

I remember the young man who attended a workshop who realized he had a "widow's mite" donor waiting to be reached out to. He did, and the organization was blessed with a large estate gift.

I know firsthand of organizations that have focused intently on big donors, ignoring the other gifts that comprise philanthropy. I have seen them reeling in times of crisis when others, who had engaged *all* of their donors, were able to keep moving forward.

And I have seen boards, those who longed for a development director to relieve them of fundraising, become even more active advocates, ambassadors, and askers as a result of a skilled professional on staff.

I hope that in this book you have discovered some ideas, truths, and tips that will help you overcome the mistakes and clear the way for your organization to be inordinately successful.

That is my wish, and was my purpose in writing it. Will we continue to make mistakes? Of course. And, we will continue to learn from them as we magnify the impact of our work in philanthropy.

George Soros, whose philanthropy has touched so many, gives us a good parting thought: "Once we realize that imperfect understanding is the human condition, there is no shame in being wrong, only in failing to correct our own mistakes."

Other Works by Kay Sprinkel Grace
Published by Emerson & Church

The Ultimate Board Member's Book
*A 1-Hour Guide to Understanding and Fulfilling
Your Role and Responsibilities, Revised Edition*
2009 • ISBN 1-889102-39-3

*Over Goal! What You Must Know to Excel
at Fundraising Today, Second Edition*
2006 • ISBN 1-889102-14-8

By Other Publishers

The AAA Way to Fundraising Success
Maximum Involvement, Maximum Results
2009 • ISBN 978-0-9720205-8-9

High Impact Philanthropy
How Donors, Boards, and Nonprofit Organizations
Can Transform Communities
2000, Co-author with Alan Wendroff
ISBN 0-471-36918-7

Beyond Fund Raising
*New Strategies for
Nonprofit Innovation and Investment*
1997 • ISBN 0471-16232-9

ABOUT THE AUTHOR Kay Sprinkel Grace, author of six books, is well-known in the U.S and internationally as an authority on fundraising, board development, and organizational management. She lives in San Francisco and is an enthusiastic photographer, traveler, and hiker. When not writing, speaking, or consulting, you can find her with her children and grandchildren who live in San Francisco, upstate New York, and France.

Copies of this and other books from the
publisher are available at discount when
purchased in quantity for boards of directors
or staff. Call 508-359-0019 or visit
www.emersonandchurch.com

Emerson
& Church
PUBLISHERS